Wrestling
Greats

GORILLA MONSOON

Ross Davies

The Rosen Publishing Group, Inc.
New York

Published in 2001 by The Rosen Publishing Group, Inc.
29 East 21st Street, New York, NY 10010

Copyright © 2001 by The Rosen Publishing Group, Inc.

First Edition

Library of Congress Cataloging-in-Publication Data

Davies, Ross.
Gorilla Monsoon / by Ross Davies.— 1st ed.
p. cm. — (Wrestling greats)
Includes bibliographical references.
ISBN 0-8239-3434-9 (lib. bdg.)
1. Gorilla Monsoon, 1937– —Juvenile literature.
2. Wrestlers—United States—Biography—Juvenile literature.
[1. Gorilla Monsoon, 1937– 2. Wrestlers.] I. Title.
GV1196.G67 D38 2001
796.812'092—dc21

                                          00-012746

Manufactured in the United States of America

Contents

Gorilla Monsoon's contributions to wrestling helped it evolve into one of the most popular sports in the United States.

"The Last I Saw of Muhammad Ali"

The date was June 5, 1976, and Gorilla Monsoon wasn't wrestling much anymore. His great professional wrestling career, which had started in 1959, was almost over. Monsoon, who loved the wrestling business more than anything else in the world, was busy with various behind-the-scenes duties at the World Wide Wrestling Federation (WWWF). But on this night in Allentown, Pennsylvania, he was wrestling. His opponent was Baron Mikel Scicluna, a German-born rulebreaker whose pleasure in hurting people angered the mild-mannered Monsoon. Before the match started, however, Monsoon looked across the ring and couldn't believe his eyes.

"What's Muhammad Ali doing here?" Monsoon said to himself. Ali was a boxer, and there was no reason for a boxer to be standing at ringside for a professional wrestling match. Monsoon quickly realized, "Ali's gotta be here to start trouble." Ali, of course, wasn't merely a boxer, but the greatest boxer in the world. He was the world heavyweight champion. Monsoon also knew that in about three weeks, Ali would step into the ring for one of his most famous matches ever: a boxer vs. wrestler match against Japanese heavyweight champion Antonio Inoki.

"Gimme a break!" Monsoon said to himself. "He's gonna do something, and I betcha it involves me!" Monsoon stopped his prematch preparation and watched. He really had no time for Ali. All he wanted to do was wrestle Scicluna, win, and get back to his hotel room for some much-needed sleep. Then the ring announcer grabbed the microphone and introduced Ali.

"Ladies and gentlemen!" he announced. "Let's have a big round of applause for the greatest boxer of all time, the heavyweight champion of the world, Muhammad Ali!" Ali stepped into the ring and waved to the crowd. The fans cheered loudly. Ali was an international hero who had been world champion for more than two years. When the applause stopped, Ali ducked out of the ring and watched as the bell was rung to start the match. "Good," Monsoon thought. "He isn't gonna do anything."

But Monsoon's hopes were short-lived. The bell rang. He and Scicluna locked up in the middle of the ring. Suddenly, Ali bounded into the ring and attacked Monsoon. The crowd gasped, shocked both by Ali's actions and by the size discrepancy between the boxer and the wrestler. Ali was considered one of

Muhammad Ali was a world champion boxer and an international hero, but he couldn't beat Gorilla Monsoon in a wrestling match.

the biggest and most agile athletes in the world, but Monsoon was at least six inches taller and more than 100 pounds heavier. The crowd realized that Monsoon, the wrestler, was bigger than one of the biggest boxers ever!

As Scicluna stepped back and happily watched the scene, Ali punched Monsoon. He ripped into him with rights and lefts that ordinarily would have floored his boxing opponents. All-time greats Joe Frazier and George Foreman had been stung by Ali's punches. "Float like a butterfly, sting like a bee" was Ali's motto, but Monsoon wasn't hurt at all. Ali's punches didn't even force him to take a step backward.

The crowd must have realized this, too: If Ali can't hurt Monsoon, who's well past his prime and has never been a world champion, then how can he expect to hurt Inoki, who's in his prime and has held several world titles? Monsoon and Ali went head-to-head. Ali tried to knock Monsoon off balance by using his speed. Ali circled and jabbed. He threw a wild right hand that glided by Monsoon's chin and struck only air. Ali kept circling, kept jabbing. Monsoon, as quick and flexible as any big man who had ever wrestled, kept ducking Ali's attack.

Finally, Monsoon decided he had played with Ali enough. After Ali missed with another right, Monsoon grabbed him around the waist and raised him above his head. The look on Ali's face said it all: He was scared out of his mind. As Monsoon spun Ali nearly seven feet above the mat, the crowd stood and roared. It was a remarkable show of strength by Monsoon. After spinning him around a few times, Monsoon smiled and slammed Ali to the mat.

The shattering sound of Ali's body hitting the mat filled the arena. Ali screamed out in pain and clutched his back with both hands. Medical personnel attended Ali. Monsoon gently stepped between the ring ropes and walked to the announcer's table. The crowd watched in stunned disbelief: Boxing's heavyweight champion of the world had been humiliated!

"Ali might be a great boxer, but he'd be nothing in a fight with a wrestler, as I've just proved," Monsoon told the television audience. "Ali's lucky. I could've broken any bone in his body if I wanted to and he'd be out of his big payday with Inoki. Ali had better start training fast. He doesn't know a wristlock from a wristwatch."

Before then, few people thought a wrestler could beat a boxer, especially the greatest boxer in the world. Now people were changing their minds. Famous sports commentator Howard Cosell declared, "In all this nonsense, there is a chance that Ali could get hurt."

Monsoon was proud of what he had done. In his mind, a great wrestler was the equal of any athlete in the world. Ali had made the gigantic mistake of trying to prove himself against a man who had a point to prove. Three weeks later at Shea Stadium in New York, Monsoon was in wrestler Andre the Giant's corner when Andre destroyed Chuck Wepner in a wrestler vs. boxer match.

About an hour later, the Ali vs. Inoki fight took place in Japan but did not live up to expectations. Inoki, fearful of Ali's punching power, stayed on the mat for most of the match and kicked at Ali's legs. Ali, perhaps mindful of the punishment he had suffered at the hands of Monsoon, didn't mount much of an attack, either. In Monsoon's mind, there was no doubt Ali was thinking about what had happened three weeks earlier. "I would've liked to have had another go with him, but he wanted no part of me," Monsoon said. "That was the last I saw of Muhammad Ali."

2 "I Can Do This!"

The man who would later be known to millions of wrestling fans as Gorilla Monsoon had a simple upbringing. He was born Robert James Marella on June 4, 1937, in Rochester, a city in upstate New York. Rochester, which sits on Lake Ontario, was a working-class city of immigrants. Marella's parents were Italian immigrants.

Robert was born big, and he stayed big. Although he had a "normal" childhood—going to school and working summer jobs to help his family—he was anything but average. In high school, he weighed 250 pounds. "I was a lot bigger than just about anybody in my school," he once told a television interviewer. "I was on the wrestling team, and, of course, I wrestled in the heavyweight division, but my opponents were never more than about two hundred pounds, and I was usually a lot taller than them, too."

He wasn't just big. He was athletic, agile, and fast, not just for his size but compared to most kids his age. He was a stand-out athlete at Thomas Jefferson High School, where he played offensive and defensive line for the football team. Marella was named to the All-City team several times. He was also a shot put and discus champion.

To no one's surprise, he was the area's heavyweight wrestling champion. By the time he graduated from high school, Marella was six-feet five-inches tall and weighed 300 pounds. He decided to attend Ithaca College, located about two hours south of Rochester.

Marella was an outstanding athlete there, too. He was one of the largest college football players of the late 1950s. He starred on the Bombers' Division III football team and played on the offensive and defensive lines. He set school records for distance in the shot put and the discus.

Marella's school records would last well into the 1960s. He starred on the wrestling team. In one meet, Marella pinned his opponent in eighteen seconds. Marella was also a fine student. He made the dean's list all four years at Ithaca and received degrees in physical education and physiotherapy.

In 1959, his senior year at Ithaca College, Marella competed in the finals of the National Collegiate Athletic Association (NCAA) wrestling championship in Ames, Iowa. He lost in the finals to Ted Ellis of Oklahoma State University. Of course, finishing second in the nation was no small feat.

Wrestling was not only Marella's favorite sport but also the one at which he performed best. He soon received national attention. He joined the United States national wrestling team for several international meets. However, future pro wrestler Dale Lewis narrowly beat him out for a spot on the 1960 United States Olympic Team.

Not making the Olympic team was a disappointment for Marella. He was also disappointed that his bad knees kept him from being drafted by the National Football League (NFL). Believing that a career in sports was no longer an option, Marella got his license to teach. Shortly after graduating from college, Marella returned to Rochester and started teaching. But teaching couldn't satisfy his thirst for competition. He missed sports.

In the late 1950s, promoters Pedro Martinez and Frank Tunney were running wrestling cards in Rochester and nearby Buffalo, New York; Toronto, Canada; and Cleveland, Ohio. Marella attended the matches in Rochester and reached two conclusions: He was bigger than most wrestlers, and Italian American wrestlers were very popular with the fans. Then he realized: "I can do this!"

Marella went to Martinez and asked for a job. Martinez took one look at this 300-pound man and said, "Kid, you've got one." Before Marella wrestled in his first match, word quickly spread around

Rochester about a local boy, the son of Italian immigrant parents, who was going to make his wrestling debut at the next card. Marella's debut at the Rochester War Memorial Auditorium attracted 6,000 fans. On average, cards at the War Memorial had been drawing about 1,500 fans! Marella was an instant hit!

For his first match, Marella changed his name to Gino Marella. His opponent was Pancho Lopez. The crowd cheered when Gino walked to the ring. But many fans wondered, "Does this guy have any athletic ability? How can a guy who's so big move around the ring?"

They got their answer in a hurry. Marella moved around the ring with the speed and agility of a man half his size. He needed less than thirty seconds to pin Lopez. Already, Marella was a fan favorite! News about him spread quickly.

Before long, Marella was wrestling and selling out cards in Buffalo, Toronto, and Cleveland. None of his matches lasted long. Most times, Marella won in less than a minute. His matches were one-sided and lacked drama. Nobody could test him. The fans loved watching him anyway, even if they got to see him only for a minute at a time. Gino Marella, the huge, clean-cut, friendly son of Italian immigrant parents, was becoming a wrestling star!

3 The Legend of Gorilla Monsoon

G ino Marella liked being loved by the fans. He enjoyed their cheers. Each night after another victory, he would go to bed with the sound of the fans' approval ringing in his ears. The fact was, Gino Marella was a very nice guy. People who met him couldn't help but like him. He had charisma. He was kind and generous.

Marella enjoyed spending his spare time working with children and charities. Every Christmas, he dressed up as Santa Claus and visited children's orphanages in Rochester. The first time he did that was in 1960. The problem was, Gino Marella was bigger than most Santa Clauses. He couldn't find a Santa suit big enough for his 300-pound body.

Finally, after much searching, Marella and his father hunted down a big enough suit. Then they ran into another major problem: The padding that Gino stuffed into his Santa suit made him much too big to fit into the family car. So Gino's father had to borrow a truck and place his son in the back.

When they arrived at the orphanage, Gino walked through the door and fell down a flight of steps!

Gino's visits to these orphanages were one of the highlights of the year for the children and for himself. But all was not well in Gino's wrestling career. His problem was unusual: He was simply unbeatable. No other professional wrestler could beat a man as big and mobile as Marella. At first, fans were fascinated with him. They loved watching him finish off opponents in short order.

After a while, however, Marella's short matches became somewhat boring. Everybody knew he was going to win. Everybody knew that after his match, he'd stand in the ring and listen to the crowd cheering for a few minutes. But there was never any drama.

That changed in 1963 when Marella went on his first wrestling tour in Japan. Wrestling has long been a popular sport in Japan. Even today, wrestling is second only to baseball in popularity. Marella was starstruck by the other wrestlers on the tour. He was the youngest foreigner in a group of wrestlers that included all-time greats Killer Kowalski, Pat O'Connor, Haystacks Calhoun, Cowboy Bob Ellis, Sandor Szabo, and Killer X.

The Japanese promoters gave Marella two colorful nicknames: the White Elephant and the Human Typhoon. One night, he wrestled Shohei "Giant" Baba, the greatest wrestler in Japan at the time.

The Japanese promoters gave Marella two colorful nicknames:

The White Elephant

and

The Human Typhoon

Marella impressed the critical Japanese fans. He used his giant swing on Baba, twirling him around the ring effortlessly as if Baba weighed 150 pounds (in reality, Baba was six-feet nine-inches tall and weighed 283 pounds). The fans were amazed. So was Baba, who managed to win the match despite the Human Typhoon's marvelous feat of strength.

Marella also impressed Killer Kowalski, one of the most famous wrestlers in the world. Kowalski introduced Marella to Bobby Davis, a top manager of rule-breakers in the WWWF. Davis was impressed, too, and recommended Marella to WWWF owner Vince Mc-Mahon Sr. Later that summer, Marella signed with the WWWF. Like the Japanese promoters, McMahon

Wrestling manager Bobby Davis recommended Gino Marella to Vince McMahon Sr.

also thought the name Gino Marella was too ordinary. He changed Gino's name to Gorilla Monsoon.

So there you have it: The true story of how Gino Marella became a professional wrestler and ultimately Gorilla Monsoon. But truth doesn't always sell in wrestling. Sometimes, promoters make up colorful stories about wrestlers in order to make fans more curious about them. That's why the legend of Gorilla Monsoon was invented.

According to this legend, the man wrestling fans came to know as Gorilla Monsoon had been born on an isolated farm in Manchuria, which is in northeastern China. His father was Russian. His mother was Italian. Their little farm barely generated enough food to feed the family. Most of the time, Monsoon went hungry. But he had heard stories about the outside world and wanted to see it for himself.

As the legend goes, Monsoon was in his late teens when a passing caravan of entertainers camped near the family's farm. The troupe of entertainers, fascinated by the young boy's size, offered him some food and water. It was the first time Monsoon had ever mingled with outsiders.

Monsoon asked these people a lot of questions. He wanted to go with them and asked them to take him along. The leader of the caravan agreed and told Monsoon to return to their camp the next morning. Monsoon, carrying nothing but his clothes, said good-bye to his parents and showed up the next morning. He became the carnival's strong man, wrestling bears and beating them easily.

A few years later, pro wrestler Buddy Rogers was on a wrestling tour of Asia. On the afternoon of one of his matches, he decided to go sightseeing. Rogers attended the carnival and saw Monsoon wrestle a bear. He was amazed by the man's strength. Afterward, he talked to Gorilla for a few minutes— through an interpreter, of course. A few weeks later, Rogers returned to the United States and recommended the young bear wrestler to the WWWF. Shortly afterward, Monsoon was signed by the WWWF and came to America.

This remarkable story was told to fans who watched the WWWF on television and attended its shows. The story made Monsoon a more mysterious figure. As far as the fans knew, Monsoon didn't speak English. He grunted. Promoters billed him as a Neanderthal-like, missing-link beast who could destroy anyone.

Bobby Davis loved showing off his weapon against stars such as Bruno Sammartino and Antonino Rocca. Monsoon destroyed one opponent after another. He beat Rocca in less than three minutes. The *Washington Post* described him as "a hirsute [hairy] Manchurian madman." The fans booed, but Gorilla Monsoon became a superstar.

Gorilla Vs. Bruno

Success came at a price for Gorilla Monsoon. The truth was, he had liked being Gino Marella. He enjoyed working with and helping children. Of course, being a good guy hadn't done much for his wrestling career. Now that he was the bad guy, fans were paying to watch him wrestle again.

But Monsoon, who was a huge man inside and outside of the ring, didn't like being an oddity. He could never blend in with the crowd. And now that he was supposedly a behemoth from Manchuria who couldn't speak English, he couldn't talk with people either.

He had to keep up appearances wherever he went. "People are afraid to meet me and ask me for an autograph," he said. "I know I am stared at on the street. I can feel it. Many times I just turn around and stare right back and they hurry off."

Monsoon didn't like scaring people. If he had things his way, he would have shook their hands and talked to them for a few minutes. He knew, however, that wrestling was a business, not just a sport, and remaining in character was good for business.

"I could always be tough," Monsoon said years later. "That was never a problem.

I was always bigger than anybody else, so that made it easy for me to manhandle my opponents. In college, my matches never lasted very long. But it was the mean part that was tough. People thought I was this mean, unapproachable guy, when nothing could have been further from the truth."

Before Monsoon's arrival in the WWWF, on May 17, 1963, Bruno Sammartino had beaten Buddy Rogers for the WWWF world heavyweight title. Ironically, Sammartino was also the son of Italian immigrants. He was also very popular. Monsoon was changing from Italian American to Manchurian to become hated, while Sammartino, an Italian American, was the most popular wrestler in America.

From a wrestling standpoint, that made perfect sense. Back then, fan favorites rarely wrestled against other fan favorites. Promoters were careful to match fan favorites against rulebreakers (also known as bad guys).

Monsoon's switch from fan favorite to mysterious rulebreaker was timely and fortunate. Fellow wrestler Buddy Rogers realized that, too. "I recognize great talent when I see it," Rogers told *Wrestling World*. "I predict a great future in wrestling for Gorilla. I personally think he can beat anybody in the country, and if I don't beat Bruno Sammartino first, he definitely will. Look, I'm an individualist and prefer to wrestle as a single. But if I had to choose a tag partner, I'd pick Gorilla. With his strength and my knowledge, we'd be unbeatable."

Monsoon was also hungry for a shot at Sammartino. "What I would like is to meet him, beat him, and become the youngest champion, even younger than he was when he won the title," Monsoon told *Wrestling World*. "Me, I'm only twenty-six. I hope I get to him before somebody else does. He's good, but he can be beat."

The rematch between Rogers and Sammartino was scheduled for October 4, 1963, at Madison Square Garden in New York City. The demand for tickets was so high, however, that the card was moved to an outdoor baseball stadium just across the river: Roosevelt Stadium in Jersey City, New

Jersey. But Rogers wasn't feeling well. He had suffered a heart attack shortly before the title match against Sammartino and still hadn't fully recovered.

Earlier, on September 16, 1963, Monsoon was scheduled to team with Rogers against Sammartino and Bobo Brazil. Rogers backed out and was replaced by Hans Mortier. With a crowd of 17,576 watching, the two teams battled to a draw.

The rivalry between Monsoon and Sammartino was getting hotter. Monsoon was getting more confident. "I didn't experience any trouble with anyone I faced in the ring," he said. "I don't think about any special punishments. However, because of my great strength, it is physically impossible for me to go through a match without hurting my opponent in some way. I never hold back. I am easily provoked. I go wild and then display sadistic tendencies."

A few weeks before his scheduled rematch against Sammartino, Rogers pulled out, citing health reasons. *The Ring*, a popular boxing and wrestling magazine, sponsored a televised tournament to choose the new number one contender for the world title. The number one contender would face Sammartino on October 4. Monsoon entered the tournament.

"There's no way I'm going to lose," Monsoon boasted. "There's nobody in the WWWF that can beat me, and that includes Sammartino. Nobody's beaten

Gorilla grips rival
Bruno Sammartino in a
powerful headlock.

me before, and they're not going to start now. I've proven that I'm unbeatable."

Gorilla was right. He destroyed everybody in the tournament in less than a minute. In the final match, he beat rulebreaker Buddy Austin in under five minutes. Monsoon was like a raging typhoon headed straight for Sammartino. Even Sammartino's most loyal fans knew he was going to be in for a tough match.

Sammartino vs. Monsoon was big news in the New York City area. More than 18,000 fans flocked to Roosevelt Stadium. They wanted to see if Sammartino could beat the "Manchurian" madman.

Monsoon wrestled a great match. He was nervous when the bell rang, but that feeling went away as he and Sammartino locked up and started going at it—the irresistible force vs. the immovable object. Sammartino and Monsoon could barely budge each other. Fans watched in fascination as the ring shook under the weight and strength of the two big men.

As the match continued, blood poured down the faces of both men. Sammartino, who had wrestled some great matches against Buddy Rogers, had never been tested like this before. Monsoon dragged his hand over his own face, saw that he was soaked in blood, and became even more enraged.

Eighteen minutes into the match, Monsoon made a critical mistake: He threw Sammartino over the top rope, an illegal move in wrestling. The referee immediately disqualified Monsoon. Sammartino was declared the winner and remained champion.

Monsoon couldn't hide his disappointment as he walked back to the dressing room. Later, he faced reporters and, through an interpreter (which, of course, wasn't really necessary), told them: "Sammartino got lucky. He's not gonna get so lucky the next time."

In his locker room, Sammartino wondered whether there would be a next time. But there would be many next times. Gorilla vs. Bruno would happen again, and again, and again.

Gorilla Vs.
the Giants

The loss to Sammartino did nothing to hurt Gorilla's career. In fact, it made him a bigger star than ever. The last time Sammartino had wrestled Buddy Rogers, he beat him in forty-seven seconds, and Rogers was considered one of the greatest wrestlers of all time. To have lasted more than eighteen minutes with Sammartino, and to have dominated most of the match, was considered a spectacular achievement for Monsoon. Sammartino was billed as "the Strongest Man in the World." "He's not the strongest man in the world," Gorilla insisted. "I am."

The rematch was held on October 21, 1963, at Madison Square Garden. A crowd of 18,969 fans packed the world's most famous arena for what figured to be a gigantic brawl. The fans weren't disappointed. Just as they had less than three weeks earlier, Sammartino and Monsoon wrestled all-out from start to finish.

Once again, the ring shook under their weight. The two rivals hated each other more than ever. Monsoon thought he had been robbed in the first match. He couldn't believe the referee had disqualified him for a simple, but nonetheless illegal, action like throwing Sammartino over the top rope. "A warning would have sufficed," manager Bobby Davis insisted. "That was a great match. The fans didn't want to see it end that way."

The fans wanted to see a clear-cut winner, but these were two well-matched rivals. Monsoon, who weighed in at 367 pounds, dominated early. Sammartino rallied and weakened Monsoon with a wristlock. Desperate to escape, Monsoon eventually spun out of the move. Monsoon slammed Sammartino to the mat. Sammartino got up and slammed Monsoon to the mat.

Then, Sammartino whipped Monsoon into the ropes, but Monsoon avoided

Sammartino's clothesline on the rebound. Sammartino again whipped Monsoon into the ropes. The two big men collided into each other. They fell to the mat with a deafening thud. The referee began to count. With twenty-one minutes and eleven seconds gone, the referee counted to ten. Both men were still lying on the mat. According to the rules, that meant the match was over. Neither wrestler had won.

His two matches against Sammartino had turned Monsoon into wrestling's most hated villain. When Monsoon wrestled fan favorite Cowboy Ron Reed, who combined good looks with an honest ring style, the fans booed loudly as Monsoon walked into the ring. Reed wore a cowboy hat and smiled at his admirers. Monsoon, clad in black trunks and sporting a dark beard, wore a scowl.

When the bell rang, Reed used his speed to keep Monsoon off balance. He landed a few forearm smashes but couldn't budge his much larger opponent. Gorilla stalked Reed. The two wrestlers came together but were separated by the referee.

Gorilla turned up his attack. He slammed Reed to the mat, then bounced off the ropes and landed on Reed. The crowd groaned. Monsoon moved in for the kill. He picked Reed up by the legs and spun him around in a move he called the Manchurian Splash. Then he tossed Reed to the mat and covered him for the pin. The victory had taken only three minutes. As Monsoon stepped out of the ring, the fans booed again.

Monsoon and Kowalski decided to form a tag team. On November 14, 1963, in Washington, DC, Monsoon and Kowalski beat Brute Bernard and Skull Murphy for the WWWF United States tag team title. Although Monsoon and Kowalski were the most hated rulebreaker tag team in the world, they respected each other. "Gorilla Monsoon is a great wrestler," Kowalski said years later. "It was an honor to have been his tag team partner."

Sammartino and Monsoon wrestled again on November 18 at Madison Square Garden in front of another sellout crowd. Just four days after his tiring tag team title victory, Monsoon didn't have the energy to hold off Sammartino. Bruno pinned him for the first time.

Monsoon was never a pushover for Sammartino. They wrestled in Philadelphia, Pittsburgh, and Washington, DC. Although Monsoon couldn't win the title, he certainly gave Sammartino some of the toughest matches of his life."When people would ask me through the years who some of the people that amazed me were, guys like Don Leo Jonathan and Kowalski and Big Bill Miller, I always mentioned Monsoon," Sammartino said years later. "For a guy at 420 pounds, it was rare a man that size could do what he did."

Monsoon and Kowalski lost the United States tag team belts to John and Chris Tolos on December 28, 1963, in Teaneck, New Jersey. Monsoon continued his assault on Sammartino. Fans were fascinated by Monsoon's size. He wore size fourteen shoes and had a twenty-two-inch neck and a sixty-inch chest. Wherever he wrestled, sellout crowds showed up to watch. Of course, it didn't hurt that Gorilla Monsoon had one of the most colorful names in wrestling history.

The fans in the 1960s loved watching big men wrestle. In March 1964, Monsoon and Bobo Brazil, who stood six-feet four-inches tall, had their famous Battle of the Giants in New York. Brazil, the fan favorite, locked up Monsoon in a full nelson. Monsoon yanked Brazil over his head to break the hold. Brazil lunged back and caught him in a vicious wrist-lock that left Gorilla gasping in pain. The action was amazingly fast and violent. Brazil was lying flat on his back with his wrist caught in Gorilla's big hands. Brazil didn't stay on his back for long. He kicked Monsoon in the head, body-slammed him across the ring, then draped him over the top rope.

The entire crowd was on its feet as Brazil moved in for the kill. He slapped Monsoon with the back of his hand. Gorilla, trapped in the corner, bit Brazil's hand. The referee tried to stop him, but Monsoon kept biting. Brazil screamed in pain, then grabbed Monsoon's left hand and tried to rip off one of his fingers. Gorilla screamed in pain, then slammed Brazil. The time limit expired. The match was declared a draw.

Typical of Gorilla's matches against Sammartino was a bout on May 11, 1964, at Madison Square Garden. The match was the longest at the Garden in years. It lasted one hour and ten minutes. Said referee Eddie Gersh: "They tired me out. I've been refereeing wrestling for seventeen years and I never had to go this far."

Sammartino and Monsoon exchanged the advantage several times during the match. There were several near-pins. At one point, both men were flat on their backs until the eight count. The match ended in a draw at the eleven o'clock curfew, but both men could have continued. Said Sammartino: "I was tired, not exhausted." Said Monsoon: "I had no idea the time was going so fast."

Monsoon grimaced as he walked back to the locker room. "I must have

Gorilla flings
wrestling legend
Hulk Hogan
across the ring.

cracked a couple of ribs, and before that I hurt my right knee," he said. Sammartino was in pain, too. "He hurt my knee and everything else," he said. "I know he hurt his ribs and I think he cracked one on me." The crowd was delighted that Sammartino was still the WWWF world champion but angry that he hadn't finished off Monsoon for good. There was no doubt: Gorilla was the most hated man in wrestling. "You know you've done your job when the little old ladies want to stab you with their knitting needles," he told the *Philadelphia Inquirer*. Gorilla was at the top of his game.

The Two Sides of Gorilla Monsoon

6

Gorilla Monsoon carefully concealed his nice side. Having established himself as a hated rulebreaker, he didn't want fans to see his kinder, gentler side, the side the orphaned kids in Rochester saw every Christmas. As far as Monsoon was concerned, the more the fans hated him, the better.

But sometimes, Gorilla couldn't hide his goodness. One night in 1964 at Madison Square Garden, Monsoon was standing near an entrance to the arena, waiting to make his entrance. Gorilla was scowling. The fans were booing. But for a reason even he couldn't recall, Monsoon looked up and saw a pretty brunette staring down at him.

Monsoon suddenly stopped scowling. He couldn't help but smile at her. And she smiled back! Right there in crowded Madison Square Garden with the fans booing, they started to talk. Her name was Maureen. They met after the match and talked some more. Gorilla and Maureen started dating. After a few months, they were married.

Gorilla and Maureen would have three children. One of those children was a son, Joseph, who would later be known to wrestling fans as referee Joey Marella. Maureen and her children saw a side of Monsoon few others were allowed to see.

"He's the best," she told *The Wrestler*. "He loves home life and can't wait to get back to the house."

"I live for Maureen and those kids," Gorilla said. Gorilla's ring career was going great. His matches against Sammartino—and there were hundreds of them—never failed to draw sellout crowds. In 1965, Sammartino and Monsoon wrestled in the first main event at Boston Garden. Monsoon slammed Sammartino through the ring. The ring collapsed, canvas and all. The match was ruled a draw.

"Do you know how many times I've come close to beating him and taking away his title?" Monsoon raged. "I can't remember how many times. And what happened when I actually beat him? They either disqualified me or picked on some stupid rule to keep me from getting the title. But I promise you one thing: Some day soon, I'm going to beat Sammartino, and they won't have any stupid rules to fall back on because I'll beat him fair and square."

Monsoon fared better in tag team matches than he did against Sammartino. In April 1965, he and partner "Cowboy" Bill Watts beat Waldo Von Erich and Gene Kiniski for the WWWF U.S. tag team title.

They held the belts for three months before losing them to Bill and Dan Miller.

Gorilla returned to Japan in September 1966 and drew sellout crowds everywhere he wrestled. He got two title shots against international heavyweight champion Shohei Baba and lost them both. Although he was a rulebreaker, Gorilla was a popular attraction in Japan.

Gorilla's feud with Sammartino continued into 1967. By that time, Bruno had been champion for four years. On February 27, a sellout crowd at Madison Square Garden watched Monsoon beat Sammartino by countout.

A month later, in front of another sellout crowd, Sammartino and Monsoon

Gorilla prepares to body-slam an opponent during a six-man tag team match at Madison Square Garden in 1968.

had been battling for ninety minutes when the eleven o'clock curfew approached. Sammartino felled Monsoon and covered him for the pin. As the referee slammed his palm to the mat for the second time, the curfew bell rang. The match was declared a draw. Sammartino and the fans couldn't believe the match hadn't been allowed to continue for one more second. "Whaddya talking about?" Monsoon screamed at the crowd. "Gorilla was beatin' the tar outta that big meatball!"

A few months later, Sammartino beat Monsoon in a Texas Death Match. In a spectacular six-man tag team match—in which each team has three men—Gorilla smashed Sammartino over the head with a chair. Sammartino was carried away on a stretcher. But minutes later, Sammartino ran back to the ring with his bloody head bandaged. The crowd went wild as Bruno slammed Monsoon for the decisive pin.

"He'll never beat me," Sammartino declared. "He doesn't have what it takes to beat me." Monsoon vs. Sammartino might not have been the longest feud in

Gorilla traumatizes Bruno Sammartino in one of their legendary feud matches.

**"He'll never beat me,"
Sammartino declared.**

wrestling history, but it was certainly one of the longest and most intense. Sammartino and Monsoon had been rivals for nearly six years when they met on February 28, 1969, at Madison Square Garden. During the match, Monsoon lifted Bruno and tossed him over the ropes. Bruno fell on the ring apron and the referee started to count. When the ref had counted to five, Bruno tried to crawl back into the ring. He made it only halfway. The referee finished counting to ten. Monsoon was declared the winner by countout.

The fans couldn't believe what they had just seen. One fan tried to attack Monsoon and was restrained by security guards. Said Sammartino: "Gorilla is not an easy man to wrestle. When you try to pick him up, it is like picking up lead. Everything about him is so big, not only his waist, but also his legs and arms."

Monsoon, however, didn't win the world title that night. To win the world title, he had to win by pinfall or submission. A countout victory wasn't good enough. The Monsoon vs. Sammartino feud had never been hotter. And then, just like that, it cooled down.

7 A Friendly Gorilla

As Gorilla Monsoon explained years later, he was tired of being booed. He was tired of being hated. And, perhaps, in a way, he was looking out for his future, too. Monsoon, like most big men, knew he couldn't wrestle forever. The strain and constant pounding of wrestling is particularly hard on a big man. Monsoon knew that one day, he might want to make his living as a wrestling executive or announcer. To do that, it wouldn't hurt to have the fans on his side.

Around the middle of 1969, Sammartino was wrestling in a televised match when he got double-teamed by two rulebreakers. Monsoon was watching from the runway leading to the ring. Those who saw him standing there thought for sure that Monsoon would help the rulebreakers. As Monsoon headed to the ring, it looked like that was about to happen. Monsoon didn't help the rulebreakers, however. He helped Sammartino. Bruno was shocked. "I don't know why he did it, but I'm glad he did," Sammartino said. "I guess I owe him one."

Shortly afterward, Monsoon was wrestling when he, too, got double-teamed by two rulebreakers. This time, Sammartino ran into the ring and saved Monsoon. A feud that had lasted six years and hundreds of matches was finally over. Monsoon and Sammartino, after trying to kill each other for so many years, shook hands.

With that, fans finally saw the other side of Monsoon. The Manchurian story line was dropped. Suddenly, Monsoon was speaking in perfect English. He had a great voice and often sang operatic arias before his matches. Monsoon loved hearing the fans' cheers. But being a fan favorite came with a high price: It meant that Monsoon wouldn't get any more title shots against Sammartino.

Instead, Monsoon became a stepping stone for wrestlers who wanted to get a shot at Sammartino. Gorilla found himself wrestling in so-called gimmick matches against other big men. One of those matches occurred in August 1969 at Boston Garden. Monsoon wrestled Haystacks Calhoun, who weighed more than 600 pounds.

Watching these two men, who weighed a combined 1,000 pounds, was a fascinating sight. Monsoon won the match by countout after Calhoun lost his temper. "I don't know how they could let it happen," Calhoun said. "They let that Monsoon do everything to me. Everybody knows I seldom lose my temper, but this was different. I swear I could have beaten Monsoon to a pulp. It was one of the few times in my life I can remember being disqualified. I shouldn't have been disqualified. Gorilla Monsoon should have been thrown out."

Monsoon also wrestled in battle royals, free-for-alls involving twenty or more wrestlers. The goal in a battle royal is to eliminate your opponents by dumping them over the top rope. The winner is the last man standing. Monsoon dominated these battle royals by throwing two, three, four, or sometimes five men into a corner, then charging at them and crushing them with his giant girth.

Monsoon also managed Pedro Morales, one of the most popular Hispanic wrestlers of the early 1970s. Gorilla was so popular that fans sometimes tried to help him in dangerous ways. One night at Madison Square Garden in 1972, King Curtis split open Monsoon's head with a bottle opener. As blood poured from Monsoon's head, a fan rushed into the ring and tried to help him. Medical personnel eventually stopped the bleeding.

Monsoon, who was unconscious, woke up in the dressing room and asked what had happened. A doctor told him. "I don't know who you are, but I want to thank you for saving my life," Monsoon said in a magazine interview. "I really don't

Gorilla menaces King Curtis, who hangs on the ropes at a match at Madison Square Garden in 1972.

remember what you look like because I was on the verge of unconsciousness when you ran into the ring to help me."

Gorilla kept winning, but his days of wrestling in main events for the world title had ended. He was getting older, and he was slowing down. Years of epic matches against Sammartino had taken their toll on his body. In mid-1972, Monsoon toured Japan and lost to Shohei Baba in the finals of a tournament.

In 1973, Monsoon was inducted into the Ithaca College Sports Hall of Fame. He became more involved in the business side of wrestling as an assistant to WWWF owner Vince McMahon Sr. In 1974, Monsoon flew to Puerto Rico and drew

Gorilla administers a brutal neck chop to Mr. Fuji at a match in Boston in 1973.

gigantic crowds for matches against Sammartino and Andre the Giant.

Eventually, Monsoon bought 10 percent of Capital Wrestling in Puerto Rico. There were occasional nights of glory for Monsoon, such as the day in June 1976 when he stood up to Muhammad Ali and showed the entire world just how tough a wrestler can be. That was not only a proud

Gorilla Monsoon is backed into the ropes by rulebreaker Nikolai Volkoff at a match in New York City in 1976.

moment for Monsoon, but a proud moment for the sport, too.

By 1977, Sammartino had lost the world title to Superstar Billy Graham, a hated rulebreaker. That meant Gorilla could once again fight in title bouts. However, he was well past his prime. He got title shots, but he lost several matches to Graham.

In 1977 and 1978, Gorilla had his final taste of wrestling glory in Puerto Rico. On July 30, 1977, in San Juan, he beat Hartford Love for the World Wrestling Council (WWC) North American title. He held the belt for nearly a year before losing it to Sammartino. But on July 22, 1978, Monsoon did something he had never done before: He pinned Bruno for a title. Sure, it was the WWC title, not the WWWF world title, but it meant a lot to Monsoon.

"We were friends by that time," Monsoon explained, "but beating Bruno that night brought back all the memories of all our matches and all the times I hadn't beaten him. At least I could always say, 'I beat Bruno Sammartino with the title on the line.'"

Bruno and Gorilla were both winding down their careers. On March 3, 1979, Monsoon lost the WWC title to Carlos Colon in Bayamon, Puerto Rico. Several months later in Philadelphia, Monsoon announced that if he lost a match to Graham, he would retire. Gorilla lost. He never wrestled again.

The Voice of the WWF

After his retirement, Gorilla Monsoon continued working behind the scenes in the WWWF. He assisted in booking, promoting, and working with wrestlers on the road for Capital Wrestling Corporation, the parent company of the WWWF. But the sport was changing rapidly.

In 1982, Vince McMahon Jr. bought the company from his father, Vince Sr., and changed the federation's name to the World Wrestling Federation (WWF). McMahon Jr. bought Monsoon's share of the company, too, and offered him a job as a television announcer. Gorilla, with his booming voice and pleasant personality, was a natural for the job.

As wrestling entered a period of raging popularity—thanks to the emergence of WWF superstar Hulk Hogan—millions of fans tuned in every week to watch the WWF. Gorilla Monsoon became the voice of the WWF. He hosted *Wrestling Challenge* and *Prime Time Wrestling*. Gorilla, with his trademark colorful suits, bow ties, and tinted sunglasses, became even more popular than he had been during his wrestling career. He was the perfect broadcast partner for such outrageous TV sidekicks as Jesse "the Body" Ventura and Bobby "the Brain" Heenan.

In 1985, the first *WrestleMania* was shown on closed-circuit television at arenas and theaters around the world. Gorilla was the announcer with Ventura at his side. "I had to literally hold him up," Monsoon recalled about Ventura. "He was so nervous, I did not think he could go on." Later that year, *Wrestling Classic* became the WWF's first pay-per-view TV event. Again, Gorilla was the announcer. His deep, booming voice and catchphrases like "Stick a fork in him—he's done," and "They're literally hanging from the rafters" were calling cards for WWF television in the 1980s.

After retiring from wrestling, Gorilla contributed to the growing popularity of the WWF as an announcer and host.

Wrestlers felt honored to have him analyze their moves. According to King Kong Bundy, "He's somebody who knows the business. A great guy, a real class act all the way." Monsoon and Ventura announced the first five *WrestleManias*.

They were the perfect team. Monsoon was the voice of the fans. Ventura was the voice of the rulebreakers. "The name of the game is to win," Gorilla said on one broadcast. In response, Ventura said, "Well, sometimes you punish, then you win!" During their *WrestleMania III* broadcast, Ventura declared, "It ain't cheatin' unless you get caught!" "Those are your rules, Jess," Monsoon replied. "No, those are

American rules," Ventura countered. "The American way!"

Heenan and Monsoon were also an entertaining team. Heenan liked to joke about what was going on in the ring. Monsoon, who knew the names of every move and every body part, wanted to call the matches straight. Their comedic interplay entertained fans around the world. Whenever Heenan tried to tell an off-color joke, Monsoon interrupted him by saying, "Will you stop already!" Of course, the verbose Heenan never stopped.

In 1994, Monsoon was inducted into the WWF Hall of Fame, along with legends Bobo Brazil and Buddy Rogers. But tragedy was just around the corner.

Joey Marella, Gorilla's son, had become a popular referee in the WWF. Gorilla loved working with his son. He had spent so many years on the road, and now he had the chance to be with Joey almost all the time. But early in the morning on July 4, 1994, Joey fell asleep at the wheel while driving on the New Jersey Turnpike. His car skidded off the road and crashed. Joey died at age thirty-one.

Those who know Monsoon best say he lost his heart for wrestling and living after Joey died. In 1995, Gorilla became WWF president, a job he would hold until 1996. But his health, and the health of his wife, kept him away from the broadcast booth for the rest of his life. At

Gorilla Monsoon mugs with wrestling fan favorite Pedro Morales, whose career he managed in the early 1970s.

WrestleMania XV on March 28, 1999, Gorilla was a judge for a match between boxer Butterbean and wrestler Bart Gunn. That night in Philadelphia, the fans cheered him for the final time.

On August 9, 1999, Monsoon suffered a mild heart attack. Monsoon had diabetes, and the heart attack worsened his condition. He was hospitalized in

Philadelphia and placed on kidney dialysis. By October, dialysis was the only thing keeping him alive. Deciding that he didn't want to live on a machine, Monsoon had himself removed from dialysis and went home. He died on October 6, 1999, in Mooresville, New Jersey. He was sixty-two years old.

Several all-time great wrestlers attended Monsoon's funeral. Vince McMahon Jr. gave a tearful eulogy and called him "one of the finest men I ever knew." A letter written by Ventura was taped to his casket. Monsoon will be remembered forever. In fact, the WWF has memorialized him with a special tribute on its Internet Web site.

"He was king at a time when matches would last for two hours, people fought for real, and wrestling was still fun," Pedro Morales said. "When you saw that big body of Gorilla Monsoon coming at you from the ropes, you feared for your life. There was nobody who knew the sport better than Gorilla Monsoon. His body slam was an act of God. If he missed, he would kill you." But of course, Gorilla Monsoon never killed anyone. In the end, he was wrestling's most gentle giant.

Glossary

aria An elaborate melody sung by a single voice and unaccompanied by other instruments.

behemoth Something of monstrous size or power.

card The list of matches in a wrestling show.

clothesline An offensive move in which the attacking wrestler sticks out his or her arm and uses it to strike the challenger in the neck. The clothesline is often executed by whipping the opponent into the ropes, then striking him or her in the neck on the rebound.

countout   A wrestler is counted out if he or she is out of the ring for twenty seconds or more. When the wrestler leaves the ring, the referee begins his or her count at one. If the wrestler is counted out, he or she is disqualified.

curfew   The official time at which a wrestling card must end. Certain states, such as New York, have had eleven o'clock curfews for wrestling cards.

disqualification   In wrestling, a wrestler can lose by disqualification if he or she uses a foreign object, refuses to obey the referee's orders, breaks the rules repeatedly, is counted out of the ring, or if another person interferes on his or her behalf. Except in the event of a double disqualification, in which both wrestlers lose, the victory is awarded to his or her opponent. In most championship matches, the belt does not change hands on a disqualification, only on a pin or submission.

epic   Extending beyond the ordinary or usual, especially in terms of size or scope.

feat A deed that is notable, especially for courage.

feud A series of matches between two wrestlers or two tag teams. Many times one wrestler will bad-mouth the other wrestler or will sneak an attack on the opponent.

foreign object An illegal object used in the ring, such as a chair or a pencil.

full nelson A wrestling hold gained from behind an opponent by thrusting the arms under the opponent's arms and clasping the hands behind the opponent's head.

gimmick   The stage personality developed by a wrestler, in order to draw attention to him or her, or to gain publicity for a match.

girth   A measure around the body, usually of someone who is larger than average size.

manager   The person responsible for overseeing a wrestler's inside-the-ring and outside-the-ring activities. Managers often take care of a wrestler's business affairs (such as signing contracts and arranging matches), and also assist with strategy.

Manchurian Splash   A wrestling move created by Monsoon. A wrestler picks up his or her opponent and spins him or her

around, and tosses the opposing wrestler
to the mat.

Neanderthal Suggesting a caveman in
appearance, mentality, or behavior.

pin When either both shoulders or both
shoulder blades are held against the mat
for three continuous seconds. A pin ends
a match.

pinfall A win achieved by a pin.

promoter The person responsible for hir-
ing and contracting the wrestlers for a card
or federation. The promoter is also responsible for deciding the matchups for a card.

rulebreaker In wrestling, a bad guy, generally someone disliked by the fans. So-called because he violates the rulebook.

sadistic Excessively cruel.

submission hold A move that makes an opponent give up without being pinned.

tag team match Match involving two teams of two or more wrestlers. Only one wrestler is allowed in the ring at a time.

For More Information

Magazines

Pro Wrestling Illustrated, The Wrestler, Inside Wrestling, Wrestle America, and *Wrestling Superstars*
London Publishing Co.
7002 West Butler Pike
Ambler, PA 19002

WCW Magazine
P.O. Box 420235

Palm Coast, FL 32142-0235.
(800) WCW-MAGS (929-6247)

WOW Magazine

McMillen Communications
P.O. Box 500
Missouri City, TX 77459-9904
(800) 310-7047
e-mail: woworder@mcmillencomm.com
Web site: http://www.wowmagazine.com

Web Sites

Dory Funk's Web Site
http://www.dory-funk.com

Professional Wrestling Online Museum
http://www.wrestlingmuseum.com

Pro Wrestling Torch Newsletter
http://www.pwtorch.com

World Championship Wrestling
http://www.wcw.com

World Wrestling Federation
http://www.wwf.com

WOW Magazine
http://www.wowmagazine.com

For Further Reading

Albano, Lou, Burt Randolph Sugar, and
   Roger Woodson. *The Complete
   Idiot's Guide to Pro Wrestling.* 2nd
   ed. New York: Alpha Books, 2000.

Archer, Jeff. *Theater in a Squared
   Circle.* New York: White-Boucke
   Publishing, 1999.

Cohen, Dan. *Wrestling Renegades:
   An In-Depth Look at Today's
   Superstars of Pro Wrestling.* New
   York: Pocket Books, 1999.

Farley, Cal, and E.L. Howe. *Two Thousand Sons: The Story of Cal Farley's Boys Ranch*. Canaan, NH: Phoenix Publishing, 1987.

Hofstede, David. *Slammin': Wrestling's Greatest Heroes and Villains*. New York: ECW Press, 1999.

Mazer, Sharon. *Professional Wrestling: Sport and Spectacle*. Jackson, MS: University Press of Mississippi, 1998.

Myers, Robert. *The Professional Wrestling Trivia Book*. Boston, MA: Popular Technology, 1999.

Sammartino, Bruno. *Bruno Sammartino: An Autobiography of Wrestling's Living Legend.* Pittsburgh: Imagine, 1990.

Works Cited

Berger, Ira, and Sheldon Widelitz. "Golden Grappler." *Italian American,* March 1977, pp. 45–49.

"Bruno Sammartino Beat 21 Opponents All in One Night." *The Wrestler*, May 1972, pp. 32–37.

Jerome, James F. "Wrestling Champ Sammartino: A Big Man at the Bank." *People*, July 1, 1974, pp. 19–21.

Kupferberg, Herbert. "The Rough (and Rich) Life of a Wrestling Champ." *Parade*, February 15, 1976, pp. 12–16.

Sammartino, Bruno. "My Three Toughest Opponents." *Wrestling World*, June 1968, pp. 55–63.

Sammartino, Bruno. "Sammartino Speaks Out." *Wrestling World*, October 1967: pp. 19–23.

Verigan, Bill. "Pedro, Bruno in Curfew Draw and All's Well." *New York Daily News*, October 2, 1972, p. 78.

Index

Photo Credits

All photos courtesy of *Pro Wrestling Illustrated* except *pp. 9, 93* © *AP/Worldwide.*

Series Design and Layout

Geri Giordano